MEXICAN TONGUE TWISTERS

TRABALENGUAS MEXICANOS

bp

Bilingual Press/Editorial Bilingüe

General Editor
  Gary D. Keller

Managing Editor
  Karen S. Van Hooft

Senior Editor
  Mary M. Keller

Assistant Editor
  Linda St. George Thurston

Editorial Board
  Juan Goytisolo
  Francisco Jiménez
  Eduardo Rivera
  Severo Sarduy
  Mario Vargas Llosa

Address:
Bilingual Review/Press
Hispanic Research Center
Arizona State University
Tempe, Arizona 85287
(602) 965-3867

MEXICAN TONGUE TWISTERS

TRABALENGUAS MEXICANOS

collected and translated by
Robert J. Haddad

with illustrations by
Tom Graham

Bilingual Press/Editorial Bilingüe
TEMPE, ARIZONA

© 1989 by Bilingual Press/Editorial Bilingüe

ISBN: 0-927534-02-9

Library of Congress Catalog Card Number: 89-81489

PRINTED IN THE UNITED STATES OF AMERICA

Cover illustration by Tom Graham

Cover design by Peter J. Hanegraaf

CONTENTS/INDICE

Dedication

This little book is dedicated to the people of
Mexico, who over the years have shared with me their
good humor and happiness. Now it's my turn . . .

Dedicatoria

Este librito está dedicado al pueblo mexicano.
Tras los años, ha compartido conmigo su buen humor
y alegría. Ahora sí me toca a mí . . .

Preface

Tongue twisters are strings of words which when spoken or repeated quickly become difficult or practically impossible to pronounce. In some cases, they have been used for teaching proper diction and preparing people for careers in public speaking. They have also been used for curing hiccups, as therapy for lisps and other speech defects, and even for testing the fit of dentures!

Although most tongue twisters correctly follow grammatical and syntactical rules, they do not always make sense or have profound philosophical implications. They are meant to tangle tongues, to jumble speech, and to be a source of fun. But tongue twisters are not just for fun; they are part of our folklore and our cultural and linguistic heritage, and as such they are worthy of being collected, documented, and preserved. Unfortunately, there exist only a very few serious works on tongue twisters, and most of these are in the English language and were compiled either in Britain or the United States. Furthermore, many of the entries in these collections are not what I would call true tongue twisters but merely limericks and anecdotes speckled with consonant and phoneme-similar words. Such is also the case in Mexico, where the few *trabalenguas* in print are found only in elementary school books. Here again, many are in nursery rhyme and limerick form or have been created by teachers for a specific classroom setting. Although some of these are perfectly valid contemporary tongue twisters, they are not anonymous and have not been (and may never be) absorbed into oral folklore. For these reasons, I have chosen not to include them here.

The Mexican people share a passion for comedy, comic relief, and good humor, and, consequently, Spanish as it is spoken in Mexico is rich in linguistic imagery. There are probably more books on humor in Mexico than in any other Spanish-speaking country, yet among all these books of sayings, limericks, proverbs, ribald tales, and jokes, there exists not one on tongue twisters.

I have reason to believe that this is the only book published to

Prefacio

Los trabalenguas son sartas de palabras difíciles (si no imposibles) de pronunciar al decirlas o repetirlas rápidamente. A veces se han empleado en clases de dicción y oratoria. También se han usado como terapia contra el ceceo involuntario y otros defectos del habla, para curar el hipo, ¡y hasta para cerciorarse de que una dentadura postiza encaje bien!

La mayoría de los trabalenguas se ajustan a las reglas de gramática y sintaxis, aunque no siempre tengan sentido o profundas implicaciones filosóficas. Su propósito es enredar lenguas, confundir el habla y hacer pasar un buen rato. Mas los trabalenguas no sólo son divertidos, sino que forman parte de nuestra herencia cultural y lingüística y, como tales, merecen coleccionarse y preservarse.

Desgraciadamente, hay poquísimos libros de trabalenguas, casi todos en inglés, de recopilaciones hechas en la Gran Bretaña y los Estados Unidos. Aun así, estas colecciones recogen alocuciones que en mi opinión no son propiamente trabalenguas, sino simplemente refranes populares o anécdotas salpicadas de aliteraciones o fonemas semejantes. Tal es el caso de México, donde los pocos trabalenguas impresos aparecen sólo en libros de enseñanza primaria, muchos de ellos en forma de nana o ronda infantil, a veces creados por educadores con propósitos pedagógicos. Aunque puedan considerarse como verdaderos trabalenguas contemporáneos, no son anónimos y no han sido—tal vez nunca serán—absorbidos dentro del folklore popular. Por estas razones he decidido no incluirlos en este compendio.

El pueblo mexicano tiene pasión por lo cómico y lo picaresco, y ese sentido del humor lo lleva a crear imágenes lingüísticas que enriquecen el idioma español. Hay probablemente más libros humorísticos en México que en ningún otro país de habla hispana; y, sin embargo, entre todas estas obras que recogen refranes, proverbios, cuentos picantes y chistes, no existe ninguna dedicada exclusivamente a las trabalenguas.

date that deals specifically with tongue twisters from Mexico. Each was collected via personal contact in the states of México, Michoacán, Guerrero, and the Federal District. During the course of my research, it became evident to me that *trabalenguas* are as much a part of Mexican life as *chiles rellenos*. Amidst slight grins and glints in their eyes, almost everyone I spoke with recalled at least one from childhood. I would like to have written more about the history and origins of these entries, but because they are a part of oral tradition, this type of information was not accessible. In this collection, translations of regionalisms and otherwise obscure Mexican words have been provided whenever possible.

I hope that through this illustrated bilingual edition these delicious bits of language will be further preserved and made more accessible to educators, children, and language lovers everywhere. May they be a source of pleasure and language fun to all that say them!

R. J. H.

Tengo la impresión de que es éste el primer libro publicado hasta la fecha que recoge únicamente trabalenguas mexicanos. Yo mismo he reunido esta colección a través de contactos personales en los estados de México, Michoacán, Guerrero y el Distrito Federal. En este proceso, se me ha hecho evidente que los trabalenguas son parte de la vida diaria y tan mexicanos como los chiles rellenos. Entre leves sonrisas y jugetón brillar de ojos, casi todos mis interlocutores recordaban algún trabalenguas de cuando eran "chamacos". Me hubiera gustado explorar más sus orígenes, pero se dificulta el acceso a las fuentes, ya que forman parte de la tradición oral del pueblo. En esta recopilación, se traducen al inglés aquellos regionalismos o modismos mexicanos tal vez desconocidos para el público en general.

Confío en que esta edición bilingüe ilustrada contribuya a conservar estos sabrosos trocitos idiomáticos y a hacerlos más accesibles a educadores, a la niñez y a los amantes del lenguaje popular. ¡Ojalá que el decirlos sea fuente inagotable de solaz y esparcimiento lingüísticos!

R. J. H.

Blandos brazos

Blandos brazos blande Brando;
Brando blandos brazos blande.

* * *

Soft arms

Brando swings his soft arms.

El bobo bebé

La nana, la nena, Nina, Nora y Nuria,
van y ven vivo al bobo bebé.
El bobo bebé vale y no bebe vino.

       *   *   *

The foolish baby

Granny, the baby girl, Nina, Nora, and Nuria
go and see the living baby fool.
The foolish baby has merit
and doesn't drink wine.

El bobo bebé *(variación)*

Lana, Lena, Lina y Lulú
van y ven al bobo bebé.
Al bobo bebé van y ven
Lana, Lena, Lina y Lulú.

* * *

The foolish baby *(variation)*

Lana, Lena, Lina, and Lulu
go and see the foolish baby.
The foolish baby they go and see,
Lana, Lena, Lina, and Lulu.

Busca el bosque Francisco

Busca el bosque Francisco,
un vasco bisco muy brusco.
Y al verlo le dijo un chusco:
¿Buscas el bosque vasco bizco?

*   *   *

Francisco looking for the forest

Francisco, a tough, cross-eyed Basque,
was looking for the forest.
And upon seeing him, a witty man asked,
"Are you looking for the forest,
cross-eyed Basque?"

La capa parda

Compre poco capa parda,
porque el que poco capa parda compra,
poco capa parda paga.

* * *

The brown cape

Buy only a few brown capes,
because he who buys only a few brown capes,
only pays for a few brown capes.

Catalina cantarina

¿Qué cántico cantarás,
Catalina cantarina?
Canta un canto que me encante,
que me encante cuando cantes.
Catalina encantadora,
¿qué cántico cantarás?

* * *

Songstress Catalina

What song will you sing,
songstress Catalina?
Sing a song that I'll enjoy,
because I like it when you sing.
Catalina, you enchanting one,
what song will you sing?

Cielo encapotado

El cielo está encapotado;
¿Quién lo desencapotará?
El que lo desencapote,
buen desencapotador será.

*   *   *

Cloudy sky

The sky is a blanket of clouds.
Who will uncloud it?
He who clears it up,
will be a great cloud clearer.

Cielo enladrillado

El cielo está enladrillado.
¿Quién lo desenladrillará?
El desenladrillador
que lo desenladrille
buen desenladrillador será.

* * *

Sky paved with bricks

The sky is paved with bricks.
Who will take them apart?
The brick remover
who takes them apart
will be a good brick remover.

Col colosal

¡Qué col colosal colocó el loco aquel
en aquel local!
¡Qué colosal col colocó en el local aquel,
aquel loco!

*   *   *

The colossal cauliflower

What a colossal cauliflower
that crazy man put in that place!

Conima y Colima

¿Conima y Colima colindan con Lima?
Ni Colima colinda con Lima,
ni colinda con Lima Conima.
¿Pero sí colindan Conima y Colima?
Tampoco Colima y Conima colindan.

*   *   *

Conima and Colima

Do Conima and Colima border on Lima?
Colima neither borders on Lima,
nor does Lima border on Conima.
But does Conima border on Colima?
No, Colima doesn't border on Conima either.

Constantinopla

El padre de Constantinopla
se quiere desconstantinopolizar.
Y aquel que lo desconstantinopolice,
buen desconstantinopolizador será.

Constantinopla (*variación*)

El arzobispo de Constantinopla
se quiere desconstantinopolizar,
y el que lo desconstantinopolice
será un buen desconstantinopolizador.

* * *

Constantinople

The priest (archbishop) from Constantinople
wants to deconstantinopolize.
And he who deconstantinopolizes him,
will be a great deconstantinopolizer.

Crespo Cleto

¿Qué crees que es un creso, Cleto?
¿Un queso de crema crasa?
¿Crees, crespo Cleto,
que el queso de crema crasa se crece?
¡Creso no es queso, cretino!
¡Créeme, crespo Cleto, créeme!
Creso es un craso que come queso crema
que no crece.

                    *   *   *

Curly Cleto

Cleto, what do you think a creso is?
A greasy piece of cream cheese?
Do you think, curly Cleto,
that greasy cream cheese can be grown?
Creso is not a piece of cheese, you imbecile!
Believe me, curly Cleto, believe me!
Creso is a crass person who eats cream cheese
that doesn't grow.

creso, m.   Croesus, a wealthy person; the last
    king of Lydia, known for his generosity.

Cuando cuentes cuentos

Cuando cuentes cuentos,
cuenta cuantos cuentos cuentas
cuando cuentas cuentos.

* * *

When you tell stories

When you tell stories
count how many stories you tell
when you tell stories.

Changos chinos

Changos chinos rechiflados
que a las changas chinas chiflan,
¡Qué bien chiflan a las changas chinas
changos chinos rechiflados!

* * *

Chinese monkeys

Crazy Chinese male monkeys
whistle at Chinese monkey girls.
How well those crazy Chinese monkeys
whistle at their Chinese monkey girls!

chiflar, tr.v. to whistle, jeer, hiss at.
rechiflado, -a (coll.) crazy, mad.

Digo Diego

Cuando digo "digo" digo "Diego",
Cuando digo "Diego" digo "digo".

*   *   *

I say Diego

When I say "digo" I say "Diego,"
When I say "Diego" I say "digo."

Doce docenas

Dicen que dan doce docenas de dulces
donde debieran dar discos dorados.
Si donde debieran dar discos dorados
dan dulces o donas,
las deudas duplican por dones mal dados.

* * *

Twelve dozen

It is said that they give out
twelve dozen candies when instead
they should give out gold records.
If where they should give out gold records
they give out candies or doughnuts instead,
debts will be doubled because of
incorrectly given gifts.

Frago el florero

El flaco florero Frago
friega y flota en el fregadero de Flora;
en el fregadero de Flora
friega y flota el flaco florero Frago.

* * *

Frago the florist

Frago the skinny florist
washes dishes and floats in Flora's washbasin;
in Flora's washbasin,
the skinny florist Frago washes dishes
and floats.

Fuensanta

Frente a la fuente de enfrente,
la frente Fuensanta frunce.
Fuensanta frunce la frente
frente a la fuente de enfrente.

*   *   *

Fuensanta

Across from the fountain up ahead,
Fuensanta raises her eyebrows.
Fuensanta raises her eyebrows
across from the fountain up ahead.

fruncir, tr.v.   to knit (eyebrows), to wrinkle
   or pucker up the forehead area.

Jimena la jacarera

Jimena la jacarera, la gitana jaranera,
jubilosa jugueteaba gorjeando la jácara,
jamando la jícama, juergueando la jícara,
y jalando la jáquima.
Jalaba, gorjeaba, juergueaba, jamaba;
jáquima, jícara, jácara y jícama.

*   *   *

Jimena the songstress

Jimena the songstress, the gypsy merrymaker,
gleefully went frolicking, warbling her jácara,
eating her jícama, having fun with her jícara,
and pulling on a bridle.
Pulling, warbling, making fun,
eating, jícara, jácara, and jícama.

jácara, f.   1. an old, ribald-type ballad of the picaresque
   genre. 2. revelers, groups of merrymakers who stroll
   the streets singing and dancing.

jacarero, -ra, m., f.   1. ballad singer. 2. gay, carefree
   person.

jaranero, -ra, m., f.   partygoer, reveler.

jícama, f. (Mex., C. Amer.)   a type of edible tuber,
   similar to a radish.

jícara, f.   a cup or small bowl made from a calabash
   gourd.

Juan Cuinto

Juan Cuinto una vez en Pinto
contó de cuentos un ciento;
y un chico dijo contento:
¡Cuánto cuento cuenta Cuinto!

* * *

Juan Cuinto

Once when he was drunk,
Juan Cuinto told over a hundred tales.
And a little boy said happily,
How many tales Cuinto tells!

en Pinto, estar uno entre Pinto y Valdemoro
  (coll.)   to be half drunk

Lenguas luengas

Lenguas luengas corren leguas;
luego la luenga lengua del lego
leguas luengas recorre.

* * *

Long tongues

Long tongues stretch for leagues;
Later, the layman's long tongue
traverses long leagues.

Lolo el lelo

"Ese Lolo es un lelo", le dijo
la Lola a don Lalo.
Pero don Lalo le dijo a la Lola,
"No, Lola, ese Lolo no es lelo, es lila".
"¿Es un lila, don Lalo, y no un lelo?"
"Sí, Lola, es un lila y no un lelo ese Lolo",
le dijo don Lalo a la Lola.

*   *   *

Foolish Lelo

"That Lelo is foolish," said Lola to don Lalo.
But don Lalo said to Lola, "No, Lola, that Lolo
is not foolish, he's stupid."
"Is he stupid, don Lelo, not foolish?"
"Yes, Lola, that Lolo is stupid, not foolish,"
don Lalo said to Lola.

lelo, m.; lila, m., f.   stupid, foolish, silly.

María Chuchena

María Chuchena su choza techaba,
y un techador que atento acechaba
le dijo: ¿Qué techas, María Chuchena?
¿Techas tu choza o techas la ajena?

*   *   *

María Chuchena

María Chuchena was putting a roof on her hut,
and a roofer who was watching carefully
said to her, What are you roofing, María Chuchena?
Are you roofing your hut or the one next door?

Marichú Morquecho

Marichú Morquecho, chocha, mocha y ducha,
por su chacha Nicha lucha como un macho.
Como un macho lucha, ducha, mocha y chocha,
por Nicha su chacha, Marichú Morquecho.

* * *

Marichú Morquecho

Marichú Morquecho, feeble, conservative,
and skillful,
fights like a macho for her girl Nicha.
Like a macho, skillful, conservative, and feeble,
fights Marichú Morquecho for Nicha, her girl.

chocho, -cha, a.   doddering (because of age), senile,
feeble.

mocho, -cha, a.   (Mex.) conservative (in politics),
staunch.

chacha, f.   abbrev. of *muchacha.*

Matute el tomatero

El tomatero Matute
mató al matutero Mota
porque notó que un tomate tomó Mota.
Por eso, por un tomate,
mató a Mota el matutero el tomatero Matute.

* * *

Matute the tomato vendor

The tomato vendor Matute
killed Mota the smuggler
because he saw Mota steal a tomato.
Because of this, over one tomato,
the tomato vendor Matute killed
Mota the smuggler.

Memo Medina

Memo Medina mima melosamente
al minino de su mamá Manuela.

*   *   *

Memo Medina

Memo Medina sweetly pets
his mother's pussycat.

Mi mamá

Mi mamá me mima mucho.

* * *

My mother

My mother spoils me a lot.

Muchos cocos

Si yo comiera muchos cocos,
muchos cocos compraría.
Pero como pocos cocos como,
pocos cocos compro.

* * *

A lot of coconuts

If I ate a lot of coconuts,
I would buy a lot of coconuts.
But since I eat few coconuts,
I buy few coconuts.

Muchos cocos *(variación)*

Yo no compro coco.
Y porque como poco coco,
poco coco compro.

*   *   *

A lot of coconuts *(variation)*

I don't buy coconuts.
Because I eat so few coconuts,
I buy very few coconuts.

El niño Núñez

En este año,
el niño Núñez engañó
al ñoño Noreña
con la piñata de antaño.

* * *

The Núñez boy

This year,
the Núñez boy
cheated timid Noreña
with last year's piñata.

ñoño, -ña, a. timid, shy, babyish.

Pablito

Pablito clavó un clavo
en la calva de un calvito;
En la calva de un calvito
clavó un clavo Pablito.

* * *

Pablito

Pablito hammered a nail
into the forehead of a little old bald man.
Into the forehead of a little old bald man,
Pablito hammered a nail.

Pancha plancha

Si Pancha plancha
con cuatro planchas,
¿con cuántas planchas
plancha Pancha?

* * *

Pancha irons

If Pancha irons
with four irons,
How many irons
does Pancha iron with?

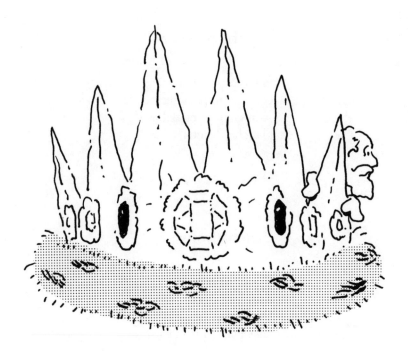

Parangaricutirimícuaro

El rey de Parangaricutirimícuaro
se quiere desparangaricutirimizar;
y quien lo desparangaricutirimice,
buen desparangaricutirimizador será.

* * *

Parangaricutirimícuaro

The king of Parangaricutirimícuaro
wants to unparangaricutirimicuarize himself.
And whoever can unparangaricutirimicuarize him,
will be a good unparangaricutirimicuarizer.

Parangaricutirimícuaro *(variación)*

Fui a Parangaricutirimícuaro
y allá me emparangaricutirimicuaricé;
quien me desemparangaricutirimicuarizare
será un gran desemparangaricutirimicuarizador.

*   *   *

Parangaricutirimícuaro *(variation)*

I went to Parangaricutirimícuaro,
and there I parangaricutirimicuarized myself.
Whoever can unparangaricutirimicuarize me
will be a great unparangaricutirimicuarizer.

La pava

Babeaba la pava, papando papeles.
La pava papaba, papeles babeando.

* * *

The turkey

The turkey was dribbling, eating papers.
The turkey was eating, papers dribbling.

Pepe Pecas

Pepe Pecas pica papas con un pico.
Con un pico pica papas Pepe Pecas.

*   *   *

Pepe Pecas

Pepe Pecas pricks potatoes with a pick.
With a pick Pepe Pecas pricks potatoes.

peca, f.   freckle.

Pepe Peplo

Pamplinoso Pepe Peplo,
una plepa pamplónica, de plomo plegó un papel.
Esa plepa, Pepe Peplo pamplinoso,
el papel plegó de plomo.

*   *   *

Pepe Peplo

Foolish Pepe Peplo,
a person from Pamplona,
folded a paper with lead.
This person, foolish Pepe Peplo,
folded the paper with lead.

La perra de Parra

Parra tenía una perra
y Guerra tenía una parra,
y que la perra de Parra
dañó la parra de Guerra.

Y Guerra cogió una porra
y le dio un porrazo a la perra
que era de Porra Parra,
y dañó la parra de Guerra.

La perra es de Parra,
la perra daño la parra,
la porra la coge Guerra,
y con la porra da a la perra de Porra,
un porrazo, Guerra.

Parra's dog

Parra had a dog
and Guerra had a grapevine,
and Parra's dog
damaged Guerra's grapevine.

So Guerra grabbed a club,
and clubbed Porra Parra's dog
who damaged Guerra's grapevine.

The dog is Parra's,
the dog damaged the grapevine,
Guerra grabs a club,
and with the club, Guerra strikes a blow
to Porra's dog.

R con R

Erre con erre cigarro,
erre con erre barril;
rápido corren los carros,
los carros del ferrocarril.

* * *

R and R

R and R, cigar
R and R, barrel;
Quickly go the cars,
the cars of the railroad train.

Rajada rueda

Recia la rajada rueda rueda rugiendo
rudamente rauda,
rauda rueda rugiendo rudamente la rajada rueda.
¡Rueda rauda, recia rueda, rauda, rauda
reciamente rueda!
¡Rueda recia, rauda rueda rugiente, rajada rueda!

* * *

The cracked wheel

Vigorously, the cracked wheel rolls,
rudely roaring rapidly.
Rapidly rolls rudely roaring the cracked wheel.
Rapidly it rolls, vigorously it rolls,
quickly, quickly it vigorously rolls!
Vigorous wheel, cracked wheel, rapidly it
rolls roaring!

Raros restos

Dos ratas, tres ratones y un robalo
son los raros restos rescatados recientemente.

* * *

Rare remains

Two rats, three mice, and a sea bass
are the rare remains rescued recently.

Reza en ruso

Ayer un premio propuso
a Rosa Rizo, Narciso,
si aprende a rezar en ruso;
y aunque un tanto confuso,
reza en ruso Rosa Rizo.

*   *   *

Pray in Russian

Yesterday, a prize was offered
to Rosa Rizo by Narciso
if she would learn to pray in Russian.
And although a bit muddled,
Rosa Rizo now prays in Russian.

Tres trastos trozados

En tres trastos trozados,
tres tristes tigres trigo trillado tragaban,
tigre tras tigre, tigre tras tigre.

* * *

Three broken bowls

In three broken bowls,
three sad tigers were eating thrashed wheat,
tiger after tiger, tiger after tiger.

Tres tristes tigres

Tres tristes tigres
tragaban trigo en tres tristes trastos.
En tres tristes trastos
tragaban trigo tres tristes tigres.

*   *   *

Three sad tigers

Three sad tigers
were gulping down wheat in three sad bowls.
In three sad bowls,
three sad tigers were gulping down wheat.

Tres tristes tigres (*variación*)

Tres tristes tigres
triscaban trigo en un trigal.
¿Qué triste tigre triscaba menos
si los tres triscaban igual?

*   *   *

Three sad tigers (*variation*)

Three sad tigers
went crushing wheat in a wheat field.
Which sad tiger crushed less
if all three crushed the same?

Viviano Bóber

Viviano Bóber bebe con el bobo,
y el bobo bebe vino,
y el que no bebe es bobo vivo.

* * *

Viviano Bóber

Viviano Bóber drinks with a fool,
and the fool drinks wine,
and he who doesn't drink is a living fool.

Yermo llano

En el yermo llano llueve llanto;
en el llano yerto llanto llueve.

* * *

Barren plains

On the barren plains it rains tears;
on the motionless plains, tears it rains.

Thank You/Gracias

Many thanks to the following people for helping me in the presentation of this book.

From Morelia, Michoacán:
Marilú Peñaloza Fabián
Dulce María Sierra Ranchel
Rafael Campos Romero

From Acapulco, Guerrero
Jesús Piñeda Díaz
Gilberto Solano López

From México, D.F.
Berta Obregón D.
Ofelia Marta Cabildo
Arturo Loreto

Spanish translation of the preface by
Raúl S. Rodríguez

Illustrations by
Tom Graham